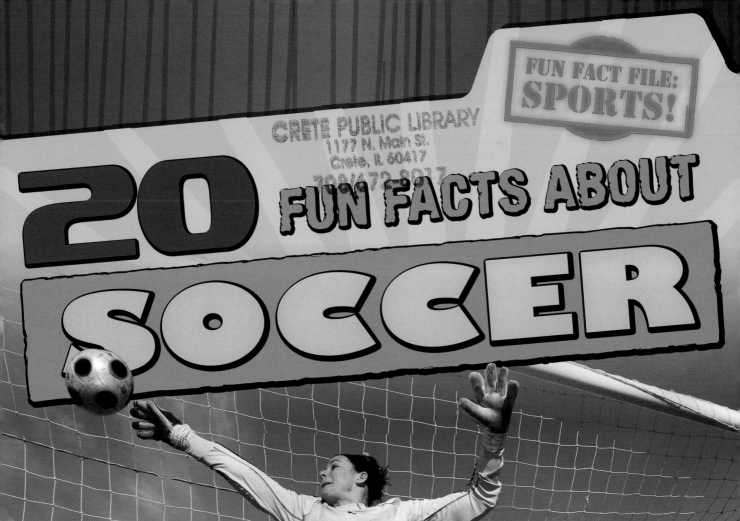

FUN FACT FILE: SPORTS!

20 FUN FACTS ABOUT SOCCER

By Ryan Nagelhout

Gareth Stevens
PUBLISHING

Please visit our website, www.garethstevens.com. For a free color catalog of all our high-quality books, call toll free 1-800-542-2595 or fax 1-877-542-2596.

Library of Congress Cataloging-in-Publication Data

Nagelhout, Ryan.
  20 fun facts about soccer / Ryan Nagelhout.
     pages cm. — (Fun fact file: Sports!)
  Includes index.
  ISBN 978-1-4824-4008-9 (pbk.)
  ISBN 978-1-4824-3981-6 (6 pack)
  ISBN 978-1-4824-3982-3 (library binding)
  1. Soccer—Miscellanea—Juvenile literature. I. Title. II. Title: Twenty fun facts about soccer.
  GV943.25.N33 2016
  796.334—dc23
                                        2015033710

First Edition

Published in 2016 by
Gareth Stevens Publishing
111 East 14th Street, Suite 349
New York, NY 10003

Copyright © 2016 Gareth Stevens Publishing

Designer: Sarah Liddell / Andrea Davison-Bartolotta
Editor: Ryan Nagelhout

Photo credits: Cover, p. 1 Stephen Mcsweeny/Shutterstock.com; p. 4 irin-k/Shutterstock.com; p. 5 muzsy/
Shutterstock.com; p. 6 Henri Rousseau/Wikimedia Commons; p. 7 Matthew Ashton - AMA/Getty Images;
p. 8 Kazuhiro Nogi/AFP/Getty Images; p. 9 Fma12/Wikimedia Commons; p. 10 John Kanuit Photography/
Sports Studio Photos/Getty Images; p. 11 Natursports/Shutterstock.com; pp. 12, 13 Maxisport/
Shutterstock.com; p. 14 Marco Luzzani/Getty Images; p. 15 Richard Laschon/Shutterstock.com; p. 16
Fabrice Coffrini/AFP/Getty Images; p. 17 Fishing4/Anadolu Agency/Getty Images; p. 18 Javier Soriano/AFP/
Getty Images; p. 19 (instant photo frames) FINDEEP/Shutterstock.com; p. 19 (top left) Gregorio Cunha/AFP/
Getty Images; p. 19 (top middle) Christof Koepsel/Bongarts/Getty Images; p. 19 (top right) Martin Bernetti/
AFP/Getty Images; p. 19 (bottom left) Philipp Schmidli/Getty Images; p. 19 (bottom middle) Steve Bardens/
Stringer/Getty Images; p. 19 (bottom right) Luis Acosta/AFP/Getty Images; p. 20 Frederic J. Brown/AFP/Getty
Images; p. 21 Hoang Dinh Nam/AFP/Getty Images; p. 22 Steve Parkin/AFP/Getty Images; p. 23
Laurence Griffiths/Getty Images; p. 24 Bob Thomas/Getty Images; p. 25 Gerard Julien/AFP/Getty Images;
p. 26 Andy Clark/AFP/Getty Images; p. 27 Stuart Franklin - FIFA/FIFA via Getty Images; p. 29 Monkey
Business Images/Shutterstock.com.

Printed in the United States of America

CPSIA compliance information: Batch #CW16GS: For further information contact Gareth Stevens, New York, New York at 1-800-542-2595.

Contents

Words in the glossary appear in **bold** type the first time they are used in the text.

Taking the Pitch

Soccer is the most popular sport in the world. Outside of the United States, soccer is often called *fútbol* or football. No matter what you call it, it's a game that's just as fun to play as it is to watch! People all over the world play this exciting game, and many more watch on TV.

There are soccer leagues all around the world, and national teams play in lots of different **tournaments**. How much do you know about soccer? Let's take a look at some amazing *fútbol* facts!

The United States isn't the only place that calls the game "soccer." Canada, Japan, and even parts of Ireland use the name as well.

5

The Name Game

The word "soccer" started as English slang for football!

Soccer is often called "**association** football" in England because rugby was often called "rugby football." The sports were called "football" because they're played on foot, not on horseback like polo. The word "association" was often shortened to "assoc," a slang term that eventually became "soccer."

Rugby football is one of the sports that American football grew out of in the 20th century.

Soccer uses lots of lingo different from other sports.

A soccer team is usually called a "club," and the names of many soccer teams include "FC," which stands for "football club." Soccer uniforms are called kits. Scoring two goals is called a "brace."

Teams that have "united" in their name were often the result of two teams merging, or coming together, to make a new team!

FACT 3

Soccer officially started in England—but similar games were played all over the world!

The Football Association was formed in England in 1863, but other games similar to soccer were played elsewhere years before. One form of soccer was played by the Han Dynasty (206 BC to AD 220) in China. Called Tsu' Chu, it featured players kicking a ball filled with feathers!

kemari

The Japanese game *kemari* has players standing in a circle kicking a ball without letting it touch the ground. It's still played today!

England has banned soccer many times.

In 1314, the Lord Mayor of London banned soccer because of the trouble the games caused in the city. During the **Hundred Years' War**, soccer was banned because the king wanted people to practice military skills, like archery, instead of the sport.

Playing soccer was banned on Sundays for hundreds of years in England due to laws of the Church of England.

9

FACT 5

Early soccer balls were made of pig bladders!

The bladder was filled with air. Each ball would be a different size and shape, depending on the bladder. The first rubber soccer ball was invented by Charles Goodyear in 1855. It had rubber panels on it that made it look like today's basketballs.

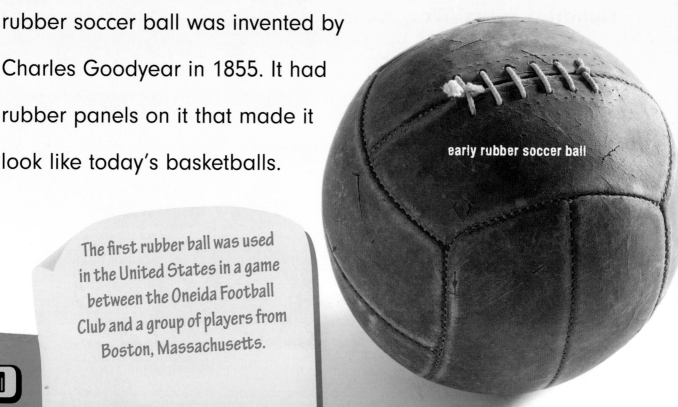

early rubber soccer ball

The first rubber ball was used in the United States in a game between the Oneida Football Club and a group of players from Boston, Massachusetts.

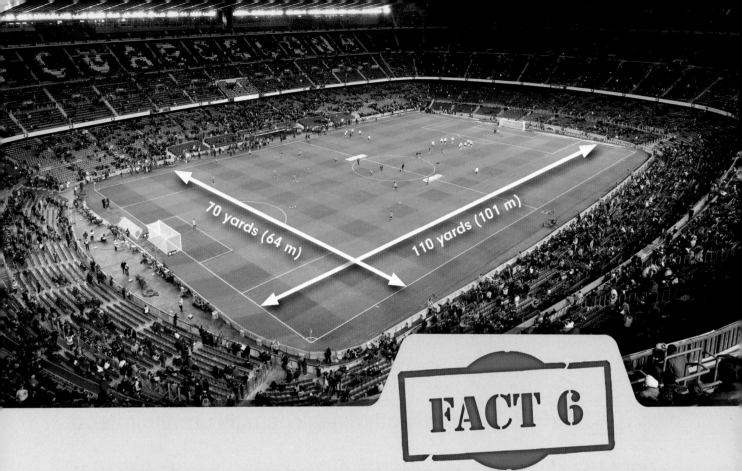

70 yards (64 m)

110 yards (101 m)

Soccer players run about 7 miles (11.3 km) during a game!

In pro soccer games, players run back and forth on fields that are at least 110 yards (101 m) long and 70 yards (64 m) wide. Midfielders have been known to run more than 9 miles (14.5 km) in a game!

Follow the Rules

FACT 7

Only keepers can touch the ball with their hands.

Keepers can only touch the ball with their hands inside their own 40-yard (36.6 m) box. Teammates can only use their head to pass back to a keeper. If teammates pass to a keeper with their feet, keepers also have to use their feet!

Keepers can always use their hands when the ball is kicked to them by the other team. That's usually when they're making a save!

The clock never stops ticking during a soccer match.

Each half is 45 minutes long. If injuries occur or the ball goes out of play, an official keeps track of the time that is lost. Minutes are added on to each half, called stoppage or "injury" time.

An official can add time on if one team wastes time or for any other reason they decide. Fans often get angry at officials for how much time they add on!

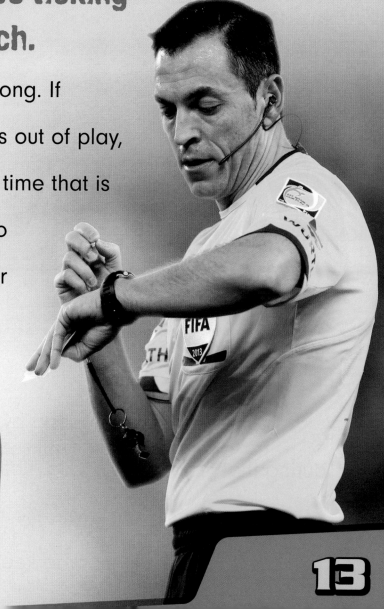

13

A yellow card is a warning, but a red card means a player has to leave the game!

FACT 9

Yellow and red foul cards weren't used until 1970!

Foul cards were first used by English **referee** Ken Alston during that year's World Cup. Referees raised the card in the air, then wrote the name of the player carded on the back to keep track of the fouls.

The Cards

Red Card

two yellow cards

dangerous play

serious fouls

out-of-control play

a foul stopping
a scoring chance in
the box

Yellow Card

not being a good sport

bad language

rough play

leaving the field
without permission

not listening to an
official

FACT 10

Switzerland is the soccer capital of the world.

FIFA was formed in 1904. "FIFA" stands for Fédération Internationale de Football Association. It was founded in Paris, France, but later moved its **headquarters** to Zurich, Switzerland. FIFA sets the rules for soccer around the world.

FIFA runs tournaments like the World Cup, which is held every 4 years.

An English team can play in the Premier League and also compete for an association's trophy, like UEFA's (Union of European Football Associations) Champions League.

FACT 11

Pro clubs can play for many different trophies.

Teams play in a domestic league, which is based in a country like England, France, or the United States. Different associations also hold tournaments throughout the season. When teams win their domestic league and their top association trophy in one season, it's called a "double"!

Going for Gold

Soccer players love playing for gold.

Many of the top prizes in soccer are gold. Both the men's and women's World Cup trophies are golden prizes given to the winner of the international tournament. A Golden Boot is often given to the top goal scorer in tournaments and leagues.

Cristiano Ronaldo

Every year, the best men's soccer player in the world is given the Ballon d'Or, French for "golden ball."

18

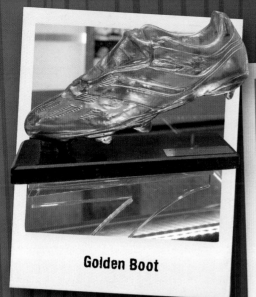
Golden Boot

World Cup trophy

Olympic Gold Medal

Soccer's Golden Goals

Ballon d'Or

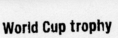
British Premier League trophy

Women's World Cup trophy

Major League Soccer

Every MLS team is owned by the league itself!

No one person or group owns a Major League Soccer (MLS) team. Owners invest in, or put money into, the league itself and are given a stake in a team. Some owners actually have stakes in multiple teams!

The MLS—the biggest soccer league in the United States—is very different from other leagues around the world.

Donovan also played for Bayern Munich in Germany and Everton in England during his career.

FACT 14

Landon Donovan is the best American player ever.

The American forward played from 2001 to 2014 with the San Jose Earthquake and LA Galaxy. Donovan finished his career with 144 goals and 136 assists, both league records. He also has the most international goals (57) in US national team history.

Player Movement

FACT 15

Players aren't traded between teams, but sold!

When one club wants a player owned by another team, they pay a **transfer fee**. The rights to the player move to the new team, and the player switches clubs. The player also signs a new contract with the new team.

Getting a new player can cost huge amounts of money! When a small club sells a player to a large club, it can often finance the small club's entire **budget** for a season!

Landon Donovan was under contract with the LA Galaxy while he was on loan to English club Everton in 2010 and 2012.

Teams can loan players to other teams if the players aren't playing well enough.

Players are still under contract with their first club, but play

for a different team. Some players are loaned to get more

playing time at a smaller club. Others are loaned because

a team doesn't want the player anymore.

Big Names

FACT 17

The "Hand of God" once scored a goal!

In the 1986 World Cup, Argentina's Diego Maradona scored a goal with his raised left hand! The goal counted and earned Maradona the nickname. Maradona also scored the "Goal of the Century" minutes later as Argentina beat England, 2-1.

Diego Maradona

Maradona's second goal was a 60-yard (55 m) sprint through five British players! It's thought to be one of the greatest goals of all time.

Other than the UEFA Champions League Final, El Clásicos are the most watched soccer matches in the world.

"El Clásico" is one of the biggest matches in soccer.

El Clásico is any match between Real Madrid and FC Barcelona, two **rival** Spanish clubs that play in the Spanish championship. Today, these matches feature two of the best players in the world—Madrid's Lionel Messi and Barca's Cristiano Ronaldo.

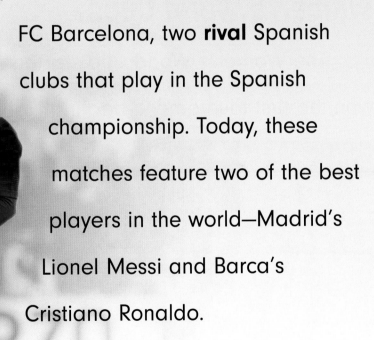

Women on the Pitch

The United States has won the most Women's World Cups.

The Women's World Cup started in 1991. The United States won the first tournament, beating Norway, 2-1. It also beat China in 1999 and Japan in 2015. The United States was runner-up to Japan in 2011.

Germany has the second-most Women's World Cup titles, winning in 2003 and 2007.

Carli Lloyd scored three goals in a Women's World Cup Final!

Lloyd scored the first hat trick in World Cup Final history, finding the net with her first three shots in the 2015 Women's World Cup Final. Lloyd scored in the third minute, the sixth minute, and the 16th minute.

The United States scored four goals in 16 minutes and beat Japan, 5-2, in the 2015 Women's World Cup Final.

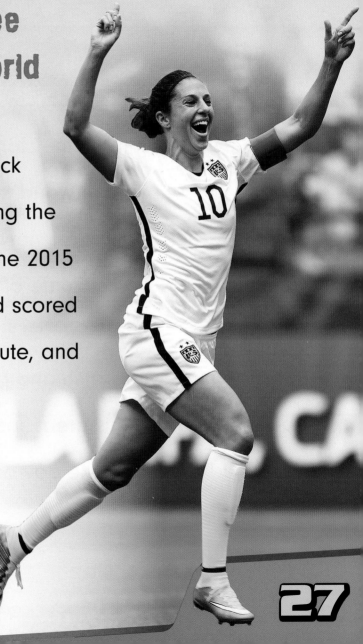

The Beautiful Game

Whether you call it soccer or football, the sport is often called the "beautiful game" for a reason. Talented players spread out all over the world make for lots of great soccer matches. There's always a new team to learn about or great new players to watch. Some of them might even join your favorite club.

The more you watch and play soccer, the more fun facts you'll learn about this great sport. Maybe you'll get to play in the World Cup Final one day or watch your favorite team win the double!

There are many different soccer leagues in the United States. Even if you don't live near an MLS team, you can always catch a game nearby!

Glossary

association: a group with similar interests

budget: the amount of money available for a purpose

dangerous: actions that put someone or something in harm's way

headquarters: the building or location where a group is based

Hundred Years' War: a war between England and France from 1337 to 1453

referee: someone who judges a game to make it fair

rival: one of two groups that compete against one another often

tournament: a contest of skill played by many different teams

transfer fee: a payment given to a club for the rights to a player

trophy: an award given for winning or doing something notable

For More Information

Books

Borth, Teddy. *Soccer: Great Moments, Records, and Facts*. Minneapolis, MN: Abdo Kids, 2015.

Jankowski, Emily. *Soccer's Greatest Records*. New York, NY: PowerKids Press, 2015.

Websites

Fédération Internationale de Football Association
fifa.com
Learn more about international soccer on the official FIFA site.

Major League Soccer
mlssoccer.com
Find out more about your favorite teams at the official site of Major League Soccer.

Premier League Soccer
premierleague.com
Learn more about England's best teams on the official BPL site.

Index